Forward:

Hello friend,

I have a confession to make. I used to think adult coloring books were just a crazy fad … really more for kids.

Maybe you did too - or still do.

Then one day, I decided to try one. I was in for a total surprise …

A friend of mine had gifted me… yep, an adult coloring book and pens! It had been gathering dust for months. Then, on one of those busy, distracted days when I was starting to feel overwhelmed, I chose the pens in the most inspiring colors I could find and started coloring in that very book.

It captured my attention, filled my senses, and calmed my mind.

It was like one of those sand paintings Tibetan Monks make on stone and marble floors … where they fill a space with their yellow and crimson robes, brilliant designs, and colors in a form of meditation.

There's something else I discovered - adult pens and pencils are a *total step up* from what many of us grew up with - although you can still reach for the Crayola, #2 pencils, or anything you like!

Try these on printer paper:

- Anything Faber-Castell
- Staedtler Ergosoft Colored Pencils
- Prismacolor Soft Core Colored Pencils
- Bear Plastic Crayons
- Copic I36B Ciao Markers

   There are so many ways you can use these!

- Relax and unwind on a break … so you can return to your work refreshed
- Reboot your energy and creativity … and get unstuck on a creative project
- As binder front-cover inserts … to add a splash of color to your home or workplace
- Frame them and put them on the wall for inspiration
- Keep the kids busy (they don't have to be for adults only!)

Still skeptical? **I double-dare you to try it.**

All my best,

Christina

Trust Your Gut

Real... not Perfect

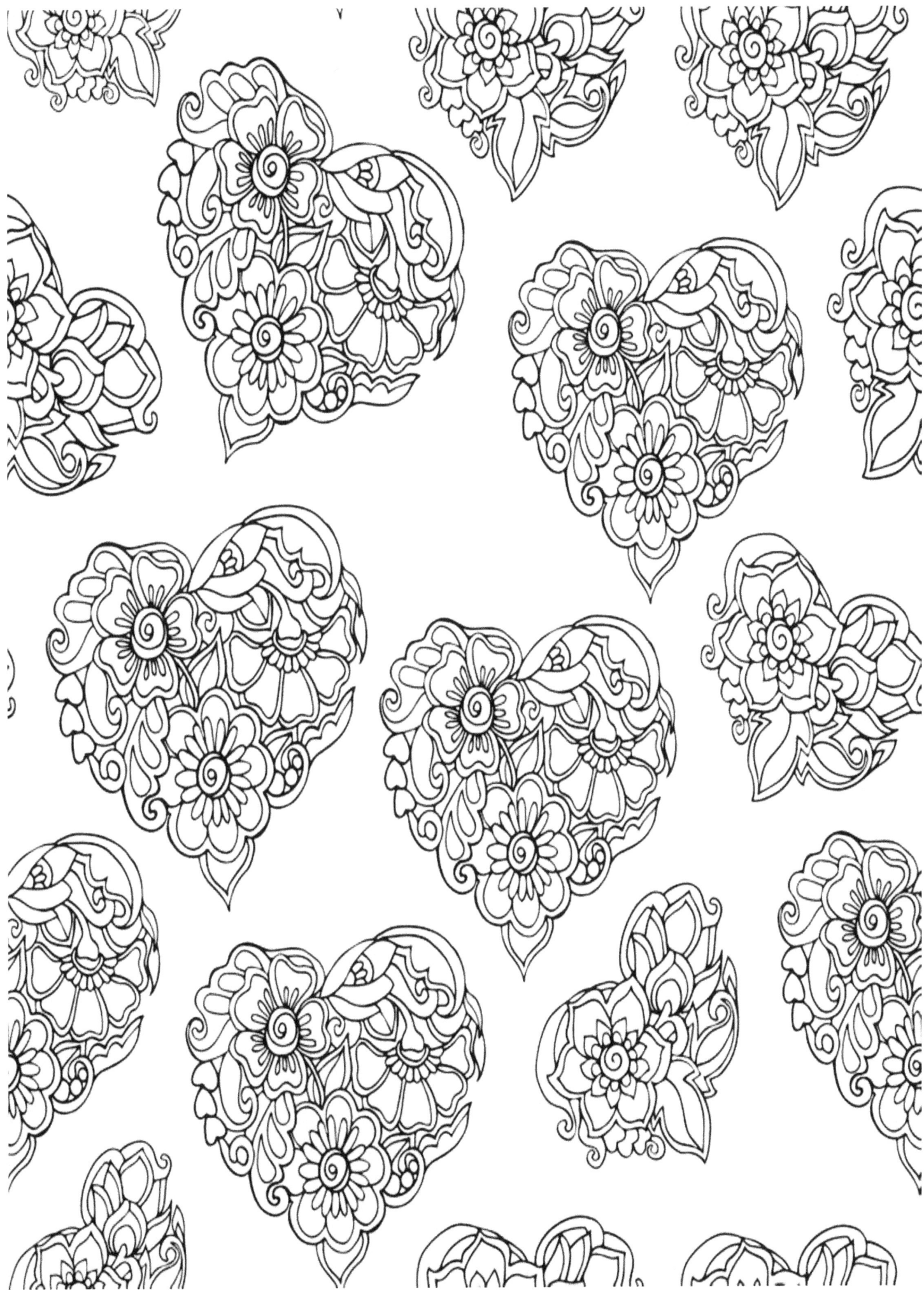

What Is
Done
In Love
Is
Done Well

-Vincent Van Gogh

YOU ARE
BROKEN
AND
BEAUTIFUL

I AM NOT AFRAID. I WAS BORN TO DO THIS.

Love Yourself First

Follow Your Bliss

you can Thrive

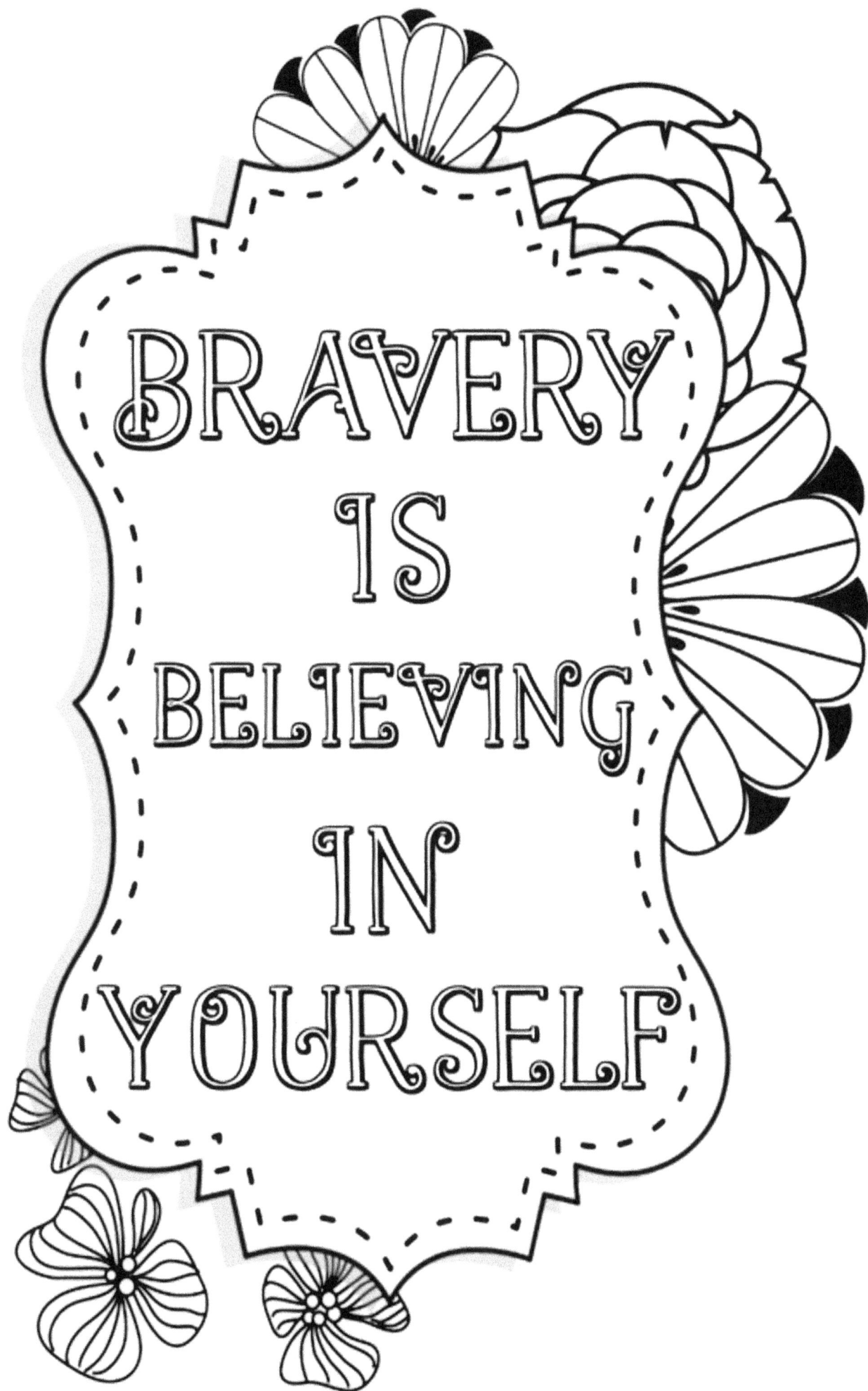

BRAVERY IS BELIEVING IN YOURSELF

COURAGE
IS GRACE
UNDER
PRESSURE

ERNEST HEMINGWAY

Wounds lead to Wisdom

BE BRAVE WITH YOUR HEART

have Hope

BE WHO YOU ARE

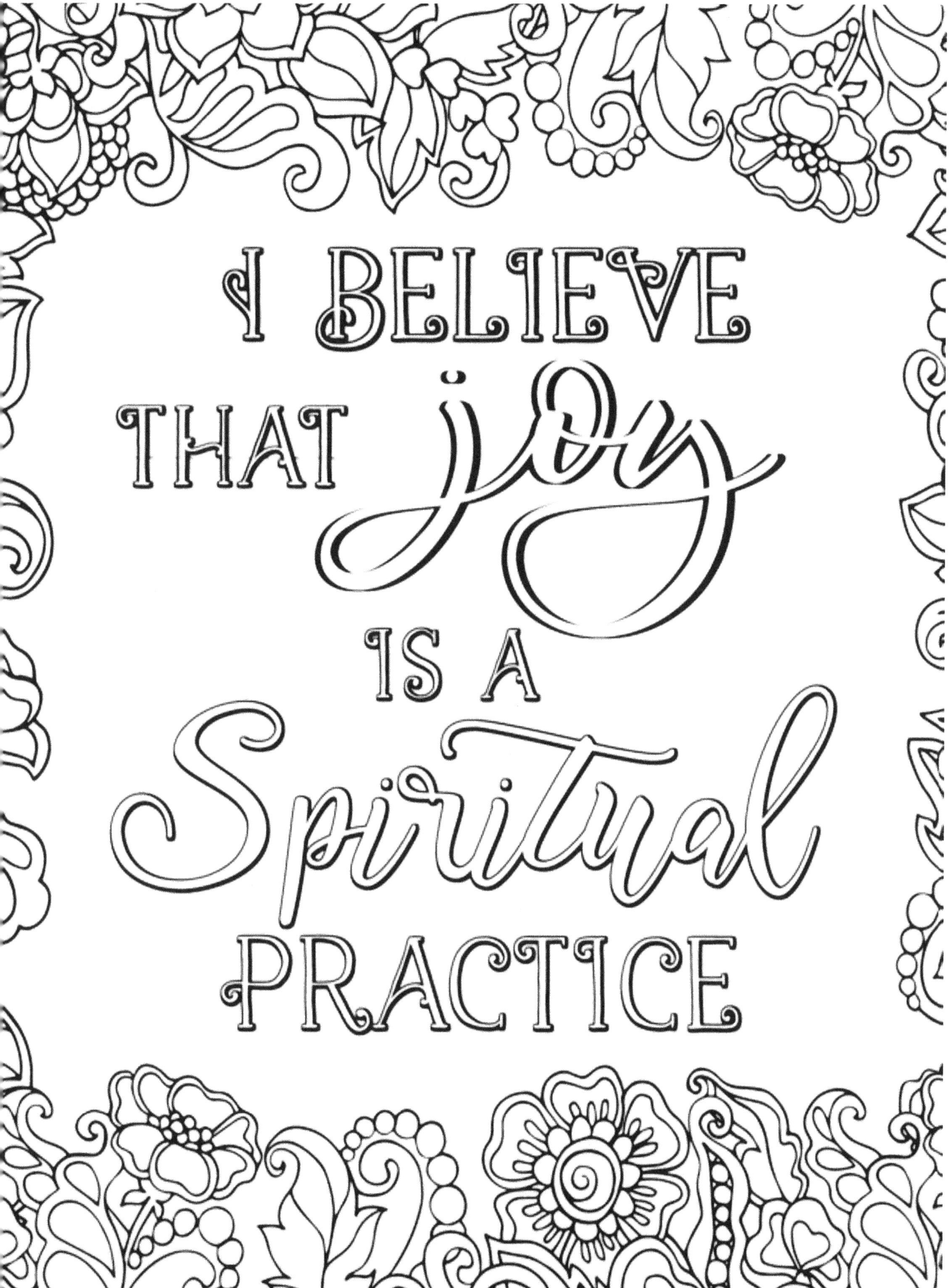
I BELIEVE
THAT joy
IS A
Spiritual
PRACTICE

dream Bigger darling

www.ingramcontent.com/pod-product-compliance
Lightning Source LLC
Chambersburg PA
CBHW081226020426
42331CB00012B/3093